The Ultimate Boogey Goo Guide & Spooky Activities for Halloween Fun

The Ultimate Boogey Goo Guide & Spooky Activities for Halloween Fun

Matthew Petchinsky

The Ultimate Boogey Goo Guide & Spooky Activities for Halloween Fun

By: Matthew Petchinsky

Welcome to the Boogey World!

Welcome, brave explorers, to the spooky, enchanting, and mysterious realm known as the **Boogey World!** In this e-book, we're about to dive into a universe full of creepy creatures, spine-tingling tales, and a whole lot of magical mischief. Whether you're looking for something to spook up your Halloween party, add some fun to a classroom event, or simply make a rainy day at home a bit more exciting, you've come to the right place.

What is the Boogey World, you ask? It's a place of imagination and curiosity where mythical boogeymen, playful monsters, and mysterious phenomena come alive! The Boogey World isn't just about scares; it's about adventure, creativity, and exploring the unknown in ways that are as thrilling as they are educational. This e-book is packed with an array of activities designed to engage the senses, tickle the imagination, and offer learning experiences that captivate kids and adults alike.

What's Inside?

In these pages, you'll find **fun, educational, and sensory activities** that bring the Boogey World to life. We've carefully crafted each activity to stimulate creativity, teach valuable lessons, and encourage hands-on interaction. There's something for everyone—whether you enjoy crafting, storytelling, experimenting, or simply getting your hands a little messy with some gooey fun.

Here's a sneak peek at what you'll explore in the Boogey World:

- **Boogeymen Identification:** Learn about the different types of boogeymen found around the world. Each chapter presents new creatures and legends, encouraging kids to imagine their own spooky beings and even create their own boogeymen using craft materials!
- **Sensory Activities:** Get your hands on some magical ingredients as we teach you how to make Boogey Goo, a delightful and kid-safe slime that is perfect for Halloween-themed sensory play.
- **Halloween Party Games:** Add an extra twist to your next Halloween bash with games inspired by boogeyman legends. From "Catch the Boogeyman" scavenger hunts to "Boogey Shuffle" dance-offs, these activities will get everyone in the party spirit.
- **Educational Crafts:** While exploring the realm of the Boogey World, children will also learn about myths, cultures, and geography. Crafting sessions include building traps for catching boogeymen, designing protective charms, and creating Boogey World maps that tell a story with every drawn line.
- **Science and Experimentation:** Embrace the curious scientist within by making your own potions and concoctions, discovering the science behind the glow-in-the-dark materials, and conducting fun experiments that reveal the secrets of the Boogey World. Each experiment includes easy-to-follow instructions and ex-

plains the science behind the magic, making it perfect for classroom events.

How to Use This Book

This book is designed to be **versatile and adaptable** for a variety of settings. Whether you're hosting a Halloween party at home, planning an educational day in the classroom, or simply seeking a fun, family-friendly activity for a rainy afternoon, you'll find activities here that fit every occasion.

- **For Halloween Parties:** Transform your gathering into an unforgettable Boogey World adventure. Use the crafts, games, and sensory activities to create a haunting atmosphere that thrills guests of all ages. Get everyone involved in making Boogey Goo, designing boogeymen masks, or embarking on a boogeyman hunt in your home or yard.
- **For Classroom Events:** Teachers and educators, this book offers a creative way to introduce students to new concepts in a fun and engaging manner. The activities can be adapted for different age groups, fostering creativity, teamwork, and learning about folklore and cultural diversity. Incorporate these sensory activities into lessons on mythology, storytelling, and even basic science.
- **For a Fun Day at Home:** Sometimes, we all need a little escape into the world of fantasy. Spend a day exploring the Boogey World from the comfort of your living room. These activities are designed to be simple and manageable, using common household items and easy-to-find craft supplies. Whether you're building a boogeyman trap, concocting a magical potion, or telling boogeyman tales by flashlight, there's fun to be had for the whole family.

A Few Words Before We Begin

Before we dive into the pages of this book, remember that the Boogey World is **all about imagination** and **creative play.** The activities are meant to be enjoyable, a little spooky, and, most importantly, adaptable to suit your unique ideas and preferences. Whether you choose to make them a little less scary for younger children or ramp up the thrill for older ones, each activity can be customized to create the perfect experience.

So, gather your supplies, don your explorer hats, and prepare to embark on an unforgettable journey through the **Boogey World!** Let's spark curiosity, promote learning, and have an absolute blast while we unravel the secrets of the boogeymen. The adventure starts here—are you ready to explore?

Chapter 1: Classic Boogey Goo (Glue-Based Slime)

Get ready to dive into the ooey-gooey world of Boogey Goo, the classic, stretchy slime that's fun to make, touch, and squish! This slime recipe is simple, easy to customize, and perfect for adding a bit of sensory magic to any Halloween party, classroom event, or a cozy day at home. Let's explore the ingredients, instructions, and tips for creating the best Boogey Goo experience!

Ingredients List

To start, you'll need some basic, **kid-friendly ingredients** to make your Boogey Goo. This recipe is **glue-based**, making it safe and simple to work with. When choosing supplies, always aim for **non-toxic** and **washable** options to ensure safe playtime fun for all ages.

- **White School Glue (4 oz bottle):** Non-toxic and washable glue is the best choice. Look for brands that specifically state they are safe for kids.
- **Baking Soda (½ teaspoon):** This acts as a thickening agent to help the slime achieve the perfect gooey consistency.
- **Contact Lens Solution (1 tablespoon):** Make sure the solution contains **boric acid** or **sodium borate**, as these are the activating agents that transform the glue into slime.
- **Water (¼ cup):** Adding a little water helps to make the slime stretchier.
- **Food Coloring:** Use kid-safe food coloring to give your Boogey Goo a spooky hue. Green, purple, orange, or black are perfect for Halloween vibes.
- **Glitter (optional):** Add some sparkle to your goo with non-toxic, kid-friendly glitter. Be sure to pick glitter that is large enough to avoid accidental ingestion.
- **Spooky Decorations (optional):** For an extra creepy twist, mix in small plastic items like googly eyes, mini spiders, or bat con-

fetti. Be sure these items are large enough that they do not pose a choking hazard for younger children.

Tips for Selecting Supplies:

- **Non-Toxic:** Always look for products labeled "non-toxic" to ensure they are safe for kids, especially since little hands might put the goo near faces.
- **Washable:** Glue, glitter, and other decorations should be easy to wash off surfaces and hands.
- **Kid-Safe Decorations:** Avoid using small or sharp objects that could be harmful. Plastic spiders, googly eyes, and foam pieces work well and add a fun touch to the slime!

Step-by-Step Instructions

Follow these easy steps to create your very own batch of classic Boogey Goo. Gather your ingredients and prepare to get a little messy!

1. **Prepare Your Workspace:** Lay down some newspaper or a plastic tablecloth to protect your working surface. Slime can be messy, so it's best to be prepared!
2. **Pour the Glue:** Empty a **4 oz bottle of white school glue** into a mixing bowl. If you want a larger batch, double the ingredients!
3. **Add Water:** Pour in **¼ cup of water** and stir to combine with the glue. This helps create a more elastic slime.
4. **Add Baking Soda:** Sprinkle in **½ teaspoon of baking soda** and mix well. The baking soda helps firm up the slime and gives it that nice stretch.
5. **Add Food Coloring:** Now it's time to add some color! Put a few drops of your chosen **food coloring** into the mixture. Stir until the color is evenly spread. If you want a darker, more intense color, add a few more drops.

Tip: To create a classic "boogeyman green," mix a few drops of green with a drop of black food coloring. For a more mystical look, try purple with a hint of glitter!

1. **Add Decorations (Optional):** If you're adding glitter or spooky decorations like googly eyes or plastic spiders, now's the time! Mix them in thoroughly to spread them evenly throughout the slime.
2. **Activate the Slime:** Slowly add **1 tablespoon of contact lens solution** to the mixture while stirring continuously. You'll notice the slime starting to form almost immediately. Keep stirring until it begins to pull away from the sides of the bowl.
3. **Knead the Slime:** Once the slime has formed, remove it from the bowl and start kneading it with your hands. This step is important for getting the right stretchy consistency. If the slime feels too sticky, add a tiny bit more contact lens solution and continue to knead.
4. **Customize Your Goo:** If you want to adjust the slime's texture, you can add a bit more contact lens solution for firmness or a few drops of water for stretchiness. Play around with the amount until you get the perfect Boogey Goo!
5. **Enjoy!** Now that your Boogey Goo is ready, let the fun begin! Stretch it, squish it, and watch it ooze as you explore the world of Boogeymen!

Tip: If you want to make multiple colors, divide the glue mixture into separate bowls before adding the food coloring.

Storage and Safety Tips

To keep your Boogey Goo fresh and safe for play, follow these storage and safety guidelines:

1. **Store in an Airtight Container:** Place your Boogey Goo in an airtight container or zip-lock bag to prevent it from drying out. It can last for several weeks if stored properly. Be sure to press out as much air as possible before sealing.

2. **Keep Cool:** Store the slime in a **cool, dry place**. Avoid direct sunlight or heat, as this can cause the slime to become too sticky or degrade faster.

3. **Clean-Up Tips:** Use warm, soapy water to wash slime off hands, clothes, and surfaces. If the slime sticks to fabrics, let it dry completely and then peel or scrape off as much as possible before washing.

4. **Safety Guidelines:**
   - **Supervise Play:** Always supervise younger children during play, especially when adding small decorations like googly eyes or plastic spiders. These items can be a choking hazard if ingested.
   - **Do Not Ingest:** Remind children that Boogey Goo is for playing, not eating. Even though the ingredients are non-toxic, the slime is not meant for consumption.
   - **Wash Hands:** Encourage kids to wash their hands before and after playing with the slime to keep it clean and free of dirt or bacteria.
   - **Allergy Check:** If a child has skin sensitivities or allergies, perform a patch test by placing a small amount of slime on the inner wrist and waiting 10 minutes to see if any reaction occurs.

5. **Disposal:** When the slime becomes too dirty or starts to lose its stretchy consistency, dispose of it in the trash. Do **not** pour it down the drain, as it can cause clogs.

Now that you've mastered the art of making classic Boogey Goo, get ready to explore even more oozy, creepy concoctions in the chapters ahead!

Boogey Goo (Glue-Free Slime Recipe)
Ingredients:

- **2 cups of cornstarch**
- **1 cup of water**
- **Food coloring** (green, purple, or black for a spooky effect)
- **Optional: glitter, small plastic eyes, or glow-in-the-dark powder** (for extra fun)

Instructions:

1. **Mix Cornstarch and Water:**
   - In a large bowl, pour 2 cups of cornstarch.
   - Gradually add 1 cup of water to the cornstarch while stirring. The mixture will become thick and gooey. Adjust the consistency by adding more cornstarch if it's too runny or more water if it's too thick.
2. **Add Color:**
   - Drop a few drops of food coloring into the mixture. Stir until the color is evenly distributed throughout the goo.
3. **Add Optional Decorations:**
   - Sprinkle in some glitter, small plastic eyes, or a bit of glow-in-the-dark powder to make the Boogey Goo look extra spooky.
4. **Play and Store:**
   - Your Boogey Goo is ready! It has a unique texture that is both solid when you press on it and liquid when you let it flow.
   - Store the Boogey Goo in an airtight container. Note that this version may dry out after a day or two, so it's best to make small batches as needed.

Safety Tips:

- This version is completely non-toxic and safe for kids. However, remind them not to ingest it and always wash hands after playing.

Why This Recipe Works

Cornstarch and water create a **non-Newtonian fluid**, meaning it behaves like both a solid and a liquid depending on how much pressure you apply. It's a fun and educational slime alternative that doesn't require glue or contact lens solution.

Chapter 2: Boogey Goo Oobleck (Glue-Free Slime)

Welcome to the next slimy chapter of the Boogey World: **Boogey Goo Oobleck!** Unlike traditional slime, this version is made without glue, making it a quick, easy, and completely safe alternative for even the youngest slime enthusiasts. Oobleck is a **non-Newtonian fluid** that changes its consistency based on how much pressure you apply, offering a fascinating sensory experience that's as much a science experiment as it is fun. Let's dive in!

Ingredients List

The best part about making Boogey Goo Oobleck is that you only need **simple pantry items** to create this creepy, gooey substance. This recipe is straightforward, kid-friendly, and requires just a few supplies:

- **Cornstarch (2 cups):** The main ingredient that gives oobleck its unique properties. Cornstarch is safe, edible, and readily available at most grocery stores.
- **Water (1 cup):** Used to mix with the cornstarch and create the oobleck's slime-like texture.
- **Food Coloring (a few drops):** To add a spooky touch, choose eerie colors like green, purple, black, or orange. Make sure to use kid-safe, non-toxic food coloring.
- **Plastic Bugs, Trinkets, or Glow-in-the-Dark Paint (optional):** Add a creepy factor to your oobleck with small plastic items like bugs or spiders. You can also mix in a bit of non-toxic glow-in-the-dark paint to make it extra spooky!

Tips for Selecting Supplies:

- **Non-Toxic:** All ingredients used in this recipe are food-safe, which means this oobleck is completely non-toxic and safe for even the littlest hands.

- **Plastic Decorations:** When adding decorations, make sure they are large enough to avoid being a choking hazard, especially for younger children.

Step-by-Step Instructions

Ready to create some ghoulish goo? Follow these simple steps to make your glue-free Boogey Goo Oobleck:

1. **Prepare Your Workspace:** Oobleck can get a bit messy, so cover your table with newspaper, a plastic tablecloth, or a large baking tray to contain the mess.
2. **Measure the Cornstarch:** In a mixing bowl, add **2 cups of cornstarch.** Cornstarch is the key ingredient that makes oobleck unique. Measure it out carefully for the best consistency.
3. **Add Food Coloring to Water:** In a separate cup, mix **1 cup of water** with a few drops of **food coloring.** For a classic boogey-man green, use green food coloring with a drop of black. For a magical twist, mix purple with a bit of glitter or glow-in-the-dark paint. Stir until the color is evenly distributed in the water.
4. **Pour the Colored Water into the Cornstarch:** Slowly pour the colored water into the bowl of cornstarch while stirring gently with a spoon or your hands. You'll notice the mixture starting to thicken as you combine the two ingredients.
5. **Mix and Adjust:** Keep stirring the mixture until it becomes hard to stir. You may need to use your hands at this point to knead and mix the oobleck. If it feels too runny, add a little more cornstarch. If it's too thick, add a few more drops of water.

Tip: Oobleck is a bit of a science experiment—its texture depends on the right balance between cornstarch and water. Adjust the ingredients as needed to achieve the perfect gooey, yet solid consistency.

1. **Customize Your Oobleck:** Once your oobleck reaches the desired consistency, it's time to add some spooky elements. Gently mix in **plastic bugs, spiders, or trinkets** for an added creepy effect. If you're using glow-in-the-dark paint, add a small amount and knead it into the oobleck to make it glow during nighttime play.
2. **Play and Explore:** Your Boogey Goo Oobleck is now ready for some spooky fun! Experiment with its unique texture by squeezing, stretching, and letting it drip through your fingers. For an extra spooky experience, dim the lights and watch the glow-in-the-dark elements come to life!

Tip: If you want to create multiple batches of oobleck in different colors, simply divide the cornstarch into smaller bowls and add differently colored water to each one.

Exploring Non-Newtonian Fluids

Oobleck isn't just fun to play with—it's also a **cool science experiment!** Oobleck is a **non-Newtonian fluid**, which means it doesn't behave like other liquids. Here's a quick and fun science explanation to share with the kids:

When you slowly dip your fingers into the oobleck, it feels soft and gooey like a liquid. But when you squeeze it, tap it, or apply quick pressure, it feels solid. That's because the cornstarch particles in the oobleck are suspended in water, creating a mixture that changes its state based on the amount of force applied.

- **Quick Pressure:** When you squeeze or punch the oobleck, the cornstarch particles press together and temporarily form a solid. This is why it feels hard when you tap or try to mold it quickly.
- **Slow Movement:** When you let it flow through your fingers slowly, the particles have time to move apart, allowing the mixture to act like a liquid and ooze around.

Why is this important? Exploring oobleck teaches kids about the fascinating properties of non-Newtonian fluids and the way different materials interact. It's a hands-on science lesson hidden inside a fun, sensory activity!

Storage and Safety Tips

Oobleck is simple to store and safe to handle, but there are a few best practices to keep in mind:

1. **Short-Term Storage:** Unlike glue-based slime, oobleck has a shorter shelf life. If you plan to keep it for a few days, store it in an airtight container. Stir it with a little water before use to refresh its texture, but it's best used on the day it's made for optimal gooiness.

2. **Clean-Up:** Oobleck can be messy, but it's easy to clean up with warm, soapy water. Allow it to dry on surfaces, then sweep or wipe it away. For clothes, let the oobleck dry completely before brushing it off and then washing the garment.

3. **Disposal:** Dispose of used oobleck in the trash. **Do not pour it down the drain** as it can solidify and cause clogs in pipes.

4. **Safety Guidelines:**
    - **Supervise Younger Children:** Always supervise young children during play, especially if you've added small plastic decorations. While oobleck is non-toxic, these decorations can pose a choking hazard.
    - **Wash Hands:** Encourage kids to wash their hands before and after playing with oobleck to keep it clean.
    - **Allergy Check:** While oobleck is made from food-safe ingredients, it's always a good idea to check for any skin sensitivities or allergies. Perform a patch test on the inner wrist if you're unsure.

By exploring the world of oobleck, kids not only get to enjoy some hands-on messy fun but also learn a bit of science along the way. Now that you've mastered glue-free Boogey Goo, you're ready for even more thrilling and gooey adventures!

Chapter 3: Boogey Slime Variations

Welcome to the world of **Boogey Slime Variations!** If you've enjoyed making classic Boogey Goo and oobleck, you're in for a treat with these new and exciting recipes. In this chapter, we'll dive into creating **soft, fluffy slime** using baking soda and hair conditioner, **glow-in-the-dark Boogey Goo** for some extra spooky fun, and an **edible Boogey Goo** that's completely safe for even the youngest kids to explore. Let's explore these diverse slime variations and bring new textures, colors, and sensations to your Boogey World adventure!

Boogey Goo with Baking Soda and Conditioner

A Soft, Fluffy Slime Recipe

This version of Boogey Goo creates a soft, fluffy slime that feels light and airy in your hands. It's easy to make, requires just two main ingredients, and results in a pleasant, moldable texture perfect for squeezing, stretching, and squishing.

Ingredients List

- **Hair Conditioner (½ cup):** Choose a non-toxic, kid-friendly conditioner with a pleasant scent. The type of conditioner will affect the texture and scent of your slime, so feel free to experiment with different options.
- **Baking Soda (1 cup):** This acts as a thickening agent to give the slime its fluffy texture. Be sure to use regular baking soda, not baking powder.
- **Food Coloring (optional):** Add a few drops of non-toxic food coloring for a fun, colorful twist. Choose spooky colors like green, purple, or orange to match the Boogey World theme.
- **Glitter and Decorations (optional):** Include glitter, foam beads, or plastic bugs for an extra eerie effect. Ensure that decorations are large enough to avoid choking hazards.

Step-by-Step Instructions

1. **Set Up Your Workspace:** Cover your table with newspaper, a plastic cloth, or a silicone mat to contain the mess. Gather all ingredients and a medium-sized mixing bowl.
2. **Mix Conditioner and Food Coloring:** Pour **½ cup of hair conditioner** into the bowl. Add a few drops of **food coloring** if you want to add color to your slime. Stir until the color is evenly distributed throughout the conditioner.
3. **Add Baking Soda:** Gradually add **1 cup of baking soda** to the conditioner. Stir the mixture with a spoon or spatula until it starts to thicken. If it becomes difficult to stir, switch to kneading with your hands to incorporate the baking soda fully.
4. **Knead the Slime:** Use your hands to knead the mixture until it transforms into a soft, fluffy slime. If it feels too sticky, add a small amount of baking soda and continue kneading. If it's too crumbly, add a little more conditioner.
5. **Customize Your Slime:** Once the slime has formed, add in **glitter, foam beads, or plastic bugs** for a spooky touch. Mix them in thoroughly until they are evenly distributed.
6. **Adjust the Texture:** If you prefer a softer, stretchier slime, add a bit more conditioner. If you want it firmer and more moldable, add a touch more baking soda. Experiment with the amounts until you achieve the desired consistency.
7. **Enjoy Your Fluffy Boogey Goo:** Your fluffy slime is now ready for play! Mold it, squish it, and stretch it into different shapes for endless fun.

Storage Tips: Store in an airtight container to keep the slime from drying out. It will usually last for about a week when stored properly.

Glow-in-the-Dark Boogey Goo
Adding a Spooky Glow to Your Slime

Take your Boogey Goo to the next level with a **glow-in-the-dark** twist! This variation works with both the classic glue-based slime and the oobleck recipe. Adding a glowing effect is perfect for nighttime play, Halloween parties, or adding a magical element to your sensory activities.

Ingredients List

- **Classic Boogey Goo Ingredients:** For this version, follow the ingredients list for either the **glue-based Boogey Goo** or **Boogey Goo Oobleck** as the base.
- **Glow-in-the-Dark Powder or Paint:** Look for non-toxic, kid-safe glow-in-the-dark powder or paint. Many craft stores carry glow-in-the-dark pigments that are safe for children's projects.

Step-by-Step Instructions

1. **Prepare Your Base:** Start by making either the classic glue-based Boogey Goo or the oobleck version. Follow the instructions in the previous chapters to create your base slime.
2. **Add Glow-in-the-Dark Powder or Paint:** Once the base slime is ready, add a small amount of **glow-in-the-dark powder** or **paint** to the mixture. For glue-based slime, mix in the powder while stirring the slime. For oobleck, sprinkle the powder onto the surface and knead it in with your hands.

Tip: If using glow-in-the-dark paint, add just a few drops and mix thoroughly to prevent the slime from becoming too sticky.

1. **Charge the Glow:** To make the slime glow, expose it to a bright light source, like a flashlight or a lamp, for a few minutes. Once

"charged," turn off the lights and watch your Boogey Goo glow eerily in the dark!

2. **Customize:** Feel free to add extra creepy elements, like plastic bugs or spiders, for an added spooky effect. The glow combined with eerie decorations creates a truly haunting Boogey World experience.

Storage Tips: Store the glow-in-the-dark Boogey Goo in an airtight container. Recharge the glow each time you play by placing the slime under a light source for a few minutes.

Edible Boogey Goo
A Safe and Tasty Slime for Younger Kids

For our youngest explorers, here's a **completely edible version** of Boogey Goo! This slime is made using safe, food-grade ingredients, so you can let little ones explore sensory play without worrying about them putting it in their mouths.

Ingredients List

- **Gelatin Slime:**
    - **Unflavored Gelatin (2 packets):** The main thickening agent for this slime.
    - **Water (1 cup):** To mix with the gelatin.
    - **Food Coloring (optional):** Non-toxic food coloring to add a fun, spooky color to the slime.
    - **Sugar (1 tablespoon):** To add a touch of sweetness.
- **Marshmallow Slime:**
    - **Mini Marshmallows (2 cups):** The main ingredient for this fluffy, stretchy slime.
    - **Cooking Oil (1 tablespoon):** To keep the slime from getting too sticky.
    - **Powdered Sugar (½ cup):** To thicken the slime and keep it from sticking.
    - **Food Coloring (optional):** Non-toxic food coloring for a fun twist.

**Step-by-Step Instructions
For Gelatin Slime:**

1. **Mix Gelatin and Water:** In a medium saucepan, mix **2 packets of unflavored gelatin** with **1 cup of water.** Stir to dissolve.
2. **Add Food Coloring:** Add a few drops of **food coloring** to the mixture and stir until evenly combined.
3. **Cook the Mixture:** Heat the mixture on low heat, stirring continuously, until the gelatin is fully dissolved and the mixture thickens slightly.
4. **Add Sugar:** Stir in **1 tablespoon of sugar** for a bit of sweetness. Continue to cook on low heat for about 2 minutes, then remove from the heat.
5. **Cool and Play:** Allow the mixture to cool for a few minutes until it's safe to touch. Knead it gently with your hands until it becomes stretchy and smooth. Now, you have an edible gelatin slime that kids can safely explore!

For Marshmallow Slime:

1. **Melt Marshmallows:** Place **2 cups of mini marshmallows** in a microwave-safe bowl. Add **1 tablespoon of cooking oil** and microwave in 20-second intervals, stirring in between, until the marshmallows are fully melted.
2. **Add Food Coloring:** Add a few drops of **food coloring** to the melted marshmallows and stir well to combine.
3. **Mix in Powdered Sugar:** Gradually add **½ cup of powdered sugar** to the melted marshmallow mixture, stirring continuously. The mixture will start to thicken and become stretchy.
4. **Knead the Slime:** Dust your hands with powdered sugar and knead the mixture until it forms a stretchy, smooth slime. If it feels too sticky, add more powdered sugar until it reaches the desired consistency.
5. **Enjoy Safe Play:** This marshmallow slime is completely edible, so kids can explore with their senses safely.

Storage Tips: Store edible Boogey Goo in an airtight container in the refrigerator. It will last for a day or two, but it's best to make fresh batches for playtime.

Safety Note: While these slimes are made with edible ingredients, always supervise young children during play to ensure safe handling.

By experimenting with these fun variations, you can introduce new textures, sensations, and even glow effects to your Boogey World adventures. Whether you're exploring the soft fluffiness of baking soda slime, the eerie glow of nighttime goo, or the completely edible slime for safe, tasty play, there's a slime recipe here for every curious explorer. Now, let's continue our journey through the Boogey World with more mysterious activities!

Chapter 4: Spooky Boogey Crafts

It's time to take the slimy fun up a notch with some **Spooky Boogey Crafts!** In this chapter, we'll create hauntingly fun crafts that bring the Boogey World to life in a whole new way. Whether it's making sensory jars filled with gooey surprises, leaving eerie "boogeyman footprints," or crafting glowing nightlights to ward off the boogeymen, these activities will spark creativity and delight. These crafts are not only perfect for Halloween but also great for classroom events and family bonding at home. Let's jump into the spooky crafting adventure!

DIY Boogey Jars

Creating Halloween-Themed Sensory Jars

Boogey Jars are sensory jars filled with slime and creepy decorations, creating a visually mesmerizing experience. Shaking, rolling, and turning these jars offer a calming sensory activity while adding a spooky Halloween twist. They're easy to make, customizable, and reusable, making them an excellent craft project for kids of all ages.

Materials List

- **Clear Plastic Jars with Lids:** Small, clear plastic jars or bottles work best for safety. Make sure the jars have secure, screw-on lids to prevent leaks.
- **Boogey Goo:** Use any of the slime recipes from previous chapters (classic glue-based, oobleck, fluffy baking soda slime) as the base for your jars.
- **Halloween Decorations:** Include small plastic spiders, bats, googly eyes, mini pumpkins, glitter, or confetti to add a spooky element.
- **Food Coloring (optional):** To color your slime for an eerie effect.
- **Glow-in-the-Dark Paint (optional):** To make the slime glow for a more mysterious look.

• **Hot Glue Gun (for adults):** To seal the jar lid securely once filled.

Step-by-Step Instructions

1. **Prepare the Slime:** Choose your favorite Boogey Goo recipe from earlier chapters and prepare the slime. For a spooky touch, add food coloring or glow-in-the-dark paint during the mixing process.
2. **Fill the Jar:** Once your slime is ready, take a clear plastic jar and fill it halfway with the slime. For an extra eerie effect, stretch and fold the slime as you place it in the jar to create folds and textures.
3. **Add Decorations:** Drop in your spooky decorations, such as plastic spiders, bats, googly eyes, and glitter. The more decorations you add, the more interesting the jar becomes. Mix in some glow-in-the-dark confetti or beads for a chilling nighttime glow.
4. **Top It Off:** Add more slime on top of the decorations to fill the jar. Leave a small space at the top to allow the contents to move around when the jar is shaken.
5. **Seal the Jar:** Close the lid tightly. To prevent leaks, use a hot glue gun to seal the edges of the lid (adult supervision required for this step). Let the glue dry completely before handling the jar.
6. **Shake and Enjoy:** Now you have your own Boogey Jar! Shake it, roll it, and watch as the slime and decorations ooze and shift, creating mesmerizing scenes inside the jar. These jars can be reused for play or kept as Halloween decorations.

Tip: Create a set of Boogey Jars using different colored slimes and decorations for a collection of eerie sensory experiences!

Boogey Footprints

Creating "Boogeyman Footprints" for a Creepy Activity

Make your Halloween night even spookier with **Boogey Footprints**—imprints left behind by the mysterious boogeymen! This activity uses a simple mixture of cornstarch and water to create eerie footprints that look as if they appeared out of nowhere. It's an interactive, sensory-rich craft that encourages imaginative play and storytelling.

Materials List

- **Cornstarch (1 cup):** The base ingredient for making the footprint mixture.
- **Water (1 cup):** To mix with the cornstarch.
- **Plastic Sheet or Baking Tray:** To create the footprints on a non-absorbent surface.
- **Paintbrush:** To paint the mixture onto feet or shoes.
- **Glow-in-the-Dark Paint (optional):** For glowing footprints in the dark.
- **Washcloths and Water:** For cleanup after the activity.

Step-by-Step Instructions

1. **Prepare Your Mixture:** In a mixing bowl, combine **1 cup of cornstarch** with **1 cup of water.** Stir the mixture until it becomes smooth and slightly thick. If you want glowing footprints, mix in a small amount of **glow-in-the-dark paint**.
2. **Set Up Your Work Area:** Lay a plastic sheet, baking tray, or wax paper on the floor or table. This will be your "footprint canvas." Make sure to use a surface that won't absorb the mixture and is easy to clean up afterward.
3. **Create the Footprints:** Using a paintbrush, apply the cornstarch mixture to the bottom of your feet or a pair of shoes. For an

extra spooky effect, you can use shoes with unusual soles to create strange footprints.

4. **Step onto the Canvas:** Step onto the plastic sheet or baking tray, leaving behind ghostly, translucent footprints. Repeat the process to create a trail of "boogeyman footprints." For an extra layer of fun, hide the footprints around the house or yard and let kids discover them during a Halloween scavenger hunt.

5. **Add a Glow:** If you used glow-in-the-dark paint in your mixture, let the footprints "charge" under a bright light. Then, turn off the lights and watch as the footprints glow mysteriously in the dark!

6. **Clean Up:** Wipe your feet or shoes with a damp washcloth after making the footprints. Dispose of the plastic sheet or rinse the baking tray to clean up the cornstarch mixture.

Tip: For an added storytelling element, combine this activity with a tale of a boogeyman creeping through the house. The glowing footprints can serve as "evidence" of its passage!

Boogey Nightlights

Crafting Glowing Nightlights Using Jars, Glow Sticks, and Stickers

Create your own **Boogey Nightlights** to keep the spooky atmosphere alive while giving a comforting glow in the dark. This craft project uses simple materials to make a glowing nightlight that doubles as a decorative Halloween piece. Customize each nightlight with stickers and glow sticks for a magical, eerie effect.

Materials List

- **Small Glass Jars or Plastic Jars:** Choose clear jars with lids to contain the glow sticks and decorations.
- **Glow Sticks:** Select glow sticks in a variety of colors. Look for kid-safe, non-toxic glow sticks to ensure safe handling.
- **Halloween Stickers or Cutouts:** Use stickers, decals, or paper cutouts of bats, ghosts, pumpkins, or other spooky shapes to decorate the outside of the jar.
- **Clear Tape or Glue (for stickers):** To attach paper cutouts if you're not using adhesive stickers.

Step-by-Step Instructions

1. **Prepare the Jar:** Clean and dry your jar thoroughly before starting. Remove any labels or stickers from the outside of the jar to ensure a clear, smooth surface.
2. **Decorate the Outside:** Attach Halloween-themed stickers or cutouts to the outside of the jar. For an eerie effect, use black silhouettes of bats, spiders, ghosts, or haunted houses. You can also use clear tape or glue to attach paper cutouts if you don't have adhesive stickers.
3. **Activate the Glow Sticks:** Bend and shake your glow sticks to activate them. You can use one color or mix different colors for

a multicolored glow. For a longer-lasting nightlight, choose glow sticks that glow for 6–8 hours.

4. **Place the Glow Sticks in the Jar:** Once activated, place the glow sticks inside the jar. Arrange them so they fit comfortably and maximize the glow effect.

5. **Seal the Jar:** Secure the lid tightly. If the glow sticks are small enough to slip through, use some clear tape around the lid's edge to ensure it stays in place.

6. **Enjoy the Glow:** Turn off the lights to watch your Boogey Nightlight come to life! The glow sticks will illuminate the jar and the Halloween stickers on the outside, creating a haunting yet comforting light.

Tip: For added fun, you can layer different glow stick colors inside the jar to create a glowing gradient effect.

Storage and Safety Tips: Keep the Boogey Nightlight out of reach of very young children to prevent them from opening the jar. Glow sticks are generally safe, but their contents should not be ingested or come into contact with skin.

With these **Spooky Boogey Crafts**, you've added another layer of magical creativity to your Boogey World experience. From sensory jars to glowing footprints and nightlights, these activities are perfect for bringing an extra dose of fun to Halloween parties, classroom events, or simply a playful evening at home. Let your imagination run wild as you craft and create, exploring the mysterious, magical world of the Boogey-man!

Ready for more eerie fun? Stay tuned as we delve deeper into the Boogey World with even more thrilling activities and adventures!

Chapter 5: Boogey-Themed Games and Activities

Welcome to the most playful part of the Boogey World—**Boogey-Themed Games and Activities!** Now that you've created all sorts of gooey slimes and spooky crafts, it's time to put them to use in games and activities that kids will love. In this chapter, you'll find exciting instructions for **Boogeyman Hide and Seek**, sensory play ideas with the various slimes you've made, and a fun **Boogey Bingo** game to play during breaks or while waiting for the goo to form. Let's dive into the spooky fun!

Boogeyman Hide and Seek

A Fun Game of Hidden Treasures in the Boogey Goo

Boogeyman Hide and Seek is a twist on the classic hide-and-seek game, involving slime and hidden trinkets. This activity combines the thrill of searching with the sensory fun of slime. Perfect for Halloween parties, classroom events, or a rainy day at home, this game is both fun and engaging for kids of all ages.

Materials Needed

- **Boogey Goo:** Use any of the slime recipes from previous chapters (classic glue-based, oobleck, fluffy baking soda slime).
- **Small Trinkets:** Choose small, safe-to-handle items like plastic spiders, mini ghosts, rubber bats, tiny skeletons, or toy gems. Make sure the trinkets are large enough to avoid choking hazards for younger children.
- **Bowls or Containers:** Large enough to hold the slime and trinkets.

Step-by-Step Instructions

1. **Prepare the Slime:** Before the game begins, make a batch of Boogey Goo using your favorite recipe. For added fun, use glow-

in-the-dark slime or add extra creepy decorations like glitter or plastic bugs to the goo.

2. **Hide the Trinkets:** While preparing the slime, hide several small trinkets inside it. Press the trinkets into the goo and fold it over to cover them. You can add as many trinkets as you like, but aim for about 5–10 items per bowl for a good balance between difficulty and fun.

3. **Explain the Game:** Gather the kids and explain that the Boogey-man has hidden treasures inside the goo, and their task is to find as many as they can. Each player will take turns digging through the slime to find the hidden trinkets.

4. **Play the Game:** One by one, let the kids dig their hands into the Boogey Goo to search for the hidden treasures. Give them a time limit (30 seconds to 1 minute) to find as many trinkets as possible. The player who finds the most trinkets wins the game!

5. **Make It Competitive:** For older kids, turn the game into a competition by setting up multiple bowls of slime with hidden trinkets. Divide the kids into teams and see which team can find all their trinkets first!

Tips:

- Use different colors of slime to create "treasure zones" where certain trinkets are worth more points.
- For an extra challenge, blindfold the players during their turn to make the search even more thrilling!

Boogey Goo Sensory Play
Creative Play Activities with Slime

Boogey Goo Sensory Play activities are perfect for children to explore the unique textures of slime while engaging their imagination and fine motor skills. These sensory games use the slimes you've made in previous chapters to provide a variety of sensory experiences that promote creativity and focus.

Sensory Play Ideas
1. Rescue the Bug

- **Materials:** Boogey Goo (classic or oobleck), plastic bugs (spiders, ants, etc.).
- **Instructions:** Hide several plastic bugs within the slime and give each child a small container. Tell them a spooky tale about how the Boogeyman trapped the bugs in his gooey lair and that they need to rescue the bugs. Let the kids dig through the slime to find and "rescue" as many bugs as they can. Once they find a bug, they place it in their container.
- **Variation:** Turn this into a timed activity. Give each child 1 minute to rescue as many bugs as possible. The child who rescues the most bugs within the time limit wins!

2. Find the Hidden Gems

- **Materials:** Boogey Goo (glow-in-the-dark works great), small plastic gems or beads.
- **Instructions:** Bury plastic gems or beads in the Boogey Goo and have the kids dig through it to find the hidden treasures. Once they've found all the gems, they can "trade" their treasures for Halloween treats or stickers.

- **Variation:** Hide a "special" gem, such as a golden bead or star. The player who finds the special gem wins a prize!

3. Shape and Sculpt

- **Materials:** Fluffy baking soda slime, plastic Halloween-themed cookie cutters (bats, pumpkins, ghosts).
- **Instructions:** Let the kids use cookie cutters to press into the slime and create spooky shapes. They can also try to sculpt their own Boogeyman creations using their hands.
- **Variation:** Hold a "slime sculpting contest" where the kids have 5 minutes to create the best Boogeyman figure. Award small prizes for the most creative sculptures.

Tips for Sensory Play:

- Always supervise young children during sensory play, especially when using small trinkets or decorations.
- Have hand wipes or a damp cloth nearby for easy clean-up after play.

Boogey Bingo

A Printable Halloween-Themed Bingo Game

Boogey Bingo is a fun, easy-to-play game that serves as the perfect break between crafting activities or while waiting for the slime to form. This bingo game has a spooky Halloween twist, featuring icons from the Boogey World like bats, pumpkins, spiders, cauldrons, ghosts, and, of course, the Boogeyman.

Materials Needed

- **Boogey Bingo Cards:** Print out the Boogey Bingo cards, each with a 5x5 grid featuring different Halloween-themed icons.
- **Bingo Markers:** Use small buttons, candy corn, or plastic spiders as markers to cover the squares on the bingo cards.
- **Caller Sheet:** A printable list of the icons featured on the bingo cards. Cut them out, fold, and place them in a small bowl for drawing during the game.
- **Prizes:** Small Halloween-themed prizes, such as stickers, plastic rings, glow sticks, or candy.
- **Get your printable board at:** https://apophisenterprisesllc.org/apophis-emporium-shop/ols/products/boogey-bingo

How to Play Boogey Bingo

1. **Prepare the Game:** Print out the Boogey Bingo cards and give one card to each player. Provide each player with a handful of markers to cover their squares. If you don't have pre-made bingo cards, you can easily create them using a bingo grid and drawing or placing small Halloween stickers in each square.
2. **Set Up the Caller:** Place the folded icons (from the caller sheet) in a small bowl. The caller will draw one icon at a time and announce it to the players.
3. **Play the Game:** The caller draws an icon from the bowl and shows it to the players. If a player has that icon on their bingo

card, they place a marker on the square. The first player to cover a row (horizontal, vertical, or diagonal) shouts "Boogey!" to win.

4. **Award Prizes:** Give the winner a small Halloween-themed prize. Then, clear the cards and play again! You can continue playing until everyone has had a chance to win a prize.

Game Variations:

- **Full Card Bingo:** For a longer game, play until a player covers their entire card.
- **Pattern Bingo:** Specify a pattern (such as an "X" or a square around the edges) that players must complete to win.

Tip: Use Halloween-themed markers, such as candy corn or mini pumpkin candies, to keep the game festive and fun.

By adding these **Boogey-Themed Games and Activities** to your Boogey World adventure, you provide kids with hours of entertainment and sensory fun. Whether they're hunting for treasures in Boogey Goo, rescuing bugs, sculpting spooky shapes, or shouting "Boogey!" during bingo, these activities are perfect for bringing imagination and laughter into playtime. So, get ready to dive into the games and let the hauntingly good times roll!

Up next, we'll continue exploring the Boogey World with even more crafts, experiments, and spooky delights!

Chapter 6: Boogey Snack Time

What's a trip to the Boogey World without some tasty treats? In this chapter, we'll explore some **Boogey Goo-themed snacks** that are not only fun to make but also safe and delicious to eat. We'll start with **gelatin-based "Boogey Goo" treats** that resemble the slime you've been crafting, followed by some quick instructions for making **Monster Marshmallow Pops**—an easy, spooky treat perfect for kids of all ages. Let's dive into the kitchen and whip up some Boogeylicious snacks!

Boogey Goo Treats

Edible Gelatin-Based Treats

These **Boogey Goo Treats** are wiggly, jiggly, and look just like the slime you've been playing with, but they're completely safe and tasty to eat! Using a gelatin base, you can create a gooey texture that's fun to stretch and squish before popping it in your mouth.

Ingredients

- **Unflavored Gelatin (2 packets):** This will give the treats their slimy texture.
- **Flavored Gelatin Mix (1 packet, any color):** Choose a spooky color like green (lime), purple (grape), or orange (orange) to match the Boogey World theme.
- **Water (2 cups):** To dissolve the gelatin.
- **Corn Syrup (2 tablespoons):** Adds a glossy, gooey texture.
- **Edible Glitter or Candy Decorations (optional):** Add some sparkle or creepy elements like candy eyes, gummy worms, or sugar skulls.

Step-by-Step Instructions

1. **Prepare the Gelatin Mixture:** In a medium saucepan, mix **2 cups of water** with the **unflavored gelatin packets**. Stir until the gelatin has dissolved.
2. **Add the Flavored Gelatin:** Add the packet of **flavored gelatin mix** to the saucepan and stir well until the mixture is smooth and all the gelatin has dissolved.
3. **Add Corn Syrup:** Stir in **2 tablespoons of corn syrup** to give the mixture a glossy, slimy texture.
4. **Add Decorations (Optional):** If you want to make your treats more fun, mix in **edible glitter** or drop in some **candy decorations** like gummy worms or candy eyes.
5. **Chill the Mixture:** Pour the gelatin mixture into a shallow dish or silicone mold. Place it in the refrigerator and let it set for about 2–3 hours or until firm.
6. **Cut into Shapes:** Once the mixture has set, use cookie cutters or a knife to cut the gelatin into fun shapes. You can also scoop it out with a spoon for a gooey effect.
7. **Serve and Enjoy:** Serve your Boogey Goo Treats on a plate or in small bowls. Kids will love the wiggly, stretchy texture and the surprise of tasty candy decorations!

Tip: For an extra spooky twist, use Halloween-themed molds to shape your treats into ghosts, pumpkins, or monsters.

Monster Marshmallow Pops
Quick and Fun Marshmallow Snacks
Monster Marshmallow Pops are a simple, no-bake treat that's perfect for kids to help create. With marshmallows, candy melts, and some spooky decorations, you can whip up these monster-themed snacks in no time.

Ingredients

- **Large Marshmallows:** The base for your monster pops.
- **Lollipop Sticks:** To hold the marshmallow pops.
- **Candy Melts (various colors):** Choose colors like green, purple, and orange for a monster theme.
- **Candy Eyes and Decorations:** For creating the monster faces. You can use candy eyes, sprinkles, mini chocolate chips, or gel icing.

Step-by-Step Instructions

1. **Prepare the Marshmallows:** Insert a **lollipop stick** into each marshmallow to create your pops. Set them aside on a tray lined with parchment paper.
2. **Melt the Candy Melts:** In a microwave-safe bowl, melt the **candy melts** according to the package instructions. Use different colors to create a variety of monster pops.
3. **Dip the Marshmallows:** Dip each marshmallow into the melted candy, covering it completely. Let the excess drip off and then place the marshmallow pop onto the parchment paper to set.
4. **Decorate the Monsters:** While the candy coating is still wet, add **candy eyes** and other decorations to create spooky monster faces. You can use sprinkles for hair, mini chocolate chips for mouths, or gel icing to add extra details.

5. **Let Them Set:** Allow the marshmallow pops to set at room temperature until the candy coating hardens (about 10–15 minutes).
6. **Serve:** Once set, your Monster Marshmallow Pops are ready to be enjoyed! Arrange them on a plate or stick them into a foam block for a spooky snack display.

Tip: For a healthier variation, use fruit slices like apple or banana slices instead of marshmallows.

Chapter 7: Boogey Goo Safety and Clean-Up Tips

Now that you've had tons of fun making slime, crafts, and snacks, it's important to know how to handle and store your Boogey Goo safely, as well as how to clean up any gooey messes. This chapter provides guidelines for **safe play**, easy **clean-up tips**, and best practices for **storing your slime** so it's ready for the next playtime.

Safe Play Guidelines

How to Handle Slime Safely, Especially with Younger Children

- **Supervision:** Always supervise young children during slime play, especially if they're using small decorations or edible slimes. Ensure they understand that some slimes are for play only and not for eating.
- **Avoid Ingestion:** Although most slimes are made with non-toxic ingredients, they are not meant to be eaten unless specifically made as edible treats. Remind children that regular slime is for squishing, not tasting.
- **Patch Test:** Before allowing extended play with slime, perform a patch test on the inner wrist to check for skin sensitivities or allergies to ingredients like glue, food coloring, or essential oils.
- **Wash Hands:** Encourage kids to wash their hands before and after slime play to keep the slime clean and avoid spreading germs.
- **Avoid Contact with Eyes:** Remind children to keep their hands away from their eyes while playing with slime to prevent irritation, especially if the slime contains small decorations or glitter.

Clean-Up Made Easy
Tips for Removing Slime from Clothes, Carpets, and Surfaces
1. From Clothes:

- **Dry and Scrape:** If slime gets on clothing, allow it to dry completely. Once dried, gently scrape off as much of the slime as possible using a spoon or the edge of a dull knife.
- **Soak:** Soak the stained area in a mixture of warm water and a bit of vinegar for 10–15 minutes to help loosen any remaining slime.
- **Wash:** After soaking, wash the clothing as usual with laundry detergent. Check the stain before drying; repeat if necessary.

2. From Carpets:

- **Scrape:** Gently scrape off as much of the slime as possible using a spoon. Be careful not to spread the slime further into the carpet fibers.
- **Vinegar Solution:** Mix equal parts of warm water and white vinegar. Dampen a clean cloth with the solution and blot the slime stain. Avoid rubbing, as this can push the slime deeper into the carpet.
- **Blot and Rinse:** Continue blotting with the vinegar solution until the slime is removed. Then, rinse the area with a clean cloth dampened with water and blot dry.

3. From Hard Surfaces:

- **Scrape:** Use a plastic scraper or spatula to lift off the slime from surfaces like tables, countertops, or floors.
- **Wipe:** Clean the area with a cloth soaked in warm soapy water. For stubborn spots, use a little vinegar on a cloth to help break down the residue.

- **Rinse and Dry:** Wipe the surface with a damp cloth to remove any remaining residue, then dry with a clean towel.

Tip: For sticky or stubborn slime stains, a bit of rubbing alcohol on a cloth can help dissolve the goo.

Storing Your Goo

Best Practices for Storing Different Types of Boogey Goo

Proper storage is key to prolonging the life of your Boogey Goo. Here's how to store different types of slime:

- **Classic Glue-Based Slime:** Store in an **airtight container** or re-sealable plastic bag to keep it from drying out. Store in a cool, dry place, away from direct sunlight or heat sources. Properly stored, this slime can last for several weeks.
- **Baking Soda and Conditioner Slime:** Place in a **resealable bag** or airtight container. This type of slime tends to dry out more quickly, so check it regularly and discard if it becomes too hard or crumbly. It usually lasts about 1 week with proper storage.
- **Oobleck:** Oobleck is best used the day it's made. If you need to store it, place it in an airtight container for up to 24 hours. Add a little water before play to refresh its texture.
- **Edible Slimes:** Store edible slimes in the refrigerator in an air-tight container. They have a shorter shelf life, usually lasting 1–2 days. Always check for signs of spoilage before allowing children to play with or eat them.

Tip: Label your containers with the date the slime was made to keep track of its freshness.

By following these safety and storage tips, you can ensure that Boogey Goo remains safe, fun, and ready for play whenever you venture back into the Boogey World! Now that you're equipped with the knowledge to handle and store your slime, get ready for more magical fun as we continue our gooey adventure!

Chapter 8: The Boogey Craft Supply List

Before diving into the Boogey World of gooey crafts, spooky snacks, and eerie games, it's essential to have all the right supplies on hand. In this chapter, we provide a **comprehensive list** of everything you'll need to create the activities, snacks, and games outlined in this book. From basic tools to ingredients for your Boogey Goo creations, this list will ensure you're fully prepared for an exciting, mess-free crafting experience. We'll also include recommendations on **where to buy** safe, child-friendly supplies so you can shop with confidence!

Essential Tools and Ingredients

A Complete List for All Your Boogey World Activities

Here's a detailed breakdown of all the **tools, ingredients, and supplies** you'll need for the various chapters and activities in this book:

1. Tools and Equipment

- **Mixing Bowls:** Medium-sized bowls for mixing slime and edible treats. Plastic or glass works best for easy cleaning.
- **Measuring Cups and Spoons:** For accurately measuring liquids and dry ingredients, including water, glue, baking soda, and cornstarch.
- **Silicone Spatulas:** Ideal for stirring and scraping slime mixtures. Silicone spatulas are easy to clean and won't stick to slime.
- **Spoons:** For mixing slime ingredients, spooning out oobleck, or spreading edible slime mixtures.
- **Plastic Trays or Baking Sheets:** Useful for containing messes during slime play and for setting up crafting stations.
- **Plastic Tablecloths or Newspapers:** To protect surfaces during messy crafting and slime-making activities.
- **Parchment Paper or Wax Paper:** For lining trays when making edible treats like Monster Marshmallow Pops.
- **Lollipop Sticks:** Used for Monster Marshmallow Pops or as stirring sticks for slime-making.

- **Cookie Cutters:** Halloween-themed cookie cutters (ghosts, pumpkins, bats) for shaping slime or edible treats.
- **Plastic Storage Containers or Resealable Bags:** For storing different types of slime, crafts, and snacks. Airtight containers help keep slime fresh for longer.
- **Hot Glue Gun (with adult supervision):** For sealing jars in crafts like DIY Boogey Jars. Use with caution and adult supervision.
- **Paintbrushes:** For applying the cornstarch mixture in Boogey Footprints and adding decorations to crafts.
- **Plastic or Glass Jars:** Clear jars for making sensory Boogey Jars and Boogey Nightlights.
- **Scissors:** For cutting materials like glow sticks, ribbons, and decorative paper.

2. Slime Ingredients

- **White School Glue:** The base ingredient for classic glue-based Boogey Goo. Choose non-toxic, washable school glue.
- **Baking Soda:** A key ingredient for fluffy slime and to help adjust slime texture.
- **Cornstarch:** Used for making oobleck and Boogey Footprints.
- **Contact Lens Solution:** Ensure it contains boric acid or sodium borate to activate the glue-based slime.
- **Hair Conditioner:** Used for making soft, fluffy Boogey Goo with baking soda. Opt for non-toxic, child-friendly conditioner.
- **Gelatin (Unflavored and Flavored):** Required for gelatin-based edible Boogey Goo Treats. The flavored gelatin adds color and flavor to the edible slime.
- **Mini Marshmallows:** The base for making edible marshmallow slime.
- **Powdered Sugar:** To thicken marshmallow slime and keep it from sticking.

- **Cooking Oil:** Prevents marshmallow slime from becoming too sticky during play.
- **Corn Syrup:** Adds a glossy, stretchy texture to gelatin-based Boogey Goo Treats.
- **Food Coloring:** Non-toxic food coloring to give your slime, crafts, and snacks a spooky appearance. Choose colors like green, purple, orange, and black.
- **Glow-in-the-Dark Powder or Paint:** Used to create glow-in-the-dark slime and footprints for an eerie effect. Choose a non-toxic variety designed for crafts.
- **Edible Glitter:** Adds sparkle to edible Boogey Goo Treats. Make sure to use food-grade glitter that is safe for consumption.

3. Decorative and Crafting Supplies

- **Plastic Spiders, Bugs, and Halloween Trinkets:** Small, child-friendly decorations to add a spooky element to slime and crafts.
- **Googly Eyes:** For adding fun, creepy faces to slime and Monster Marshmallow Pops.
- **Glitter:** Choose non-toxic, child-friendly glitter for adding sparkle to slime and sensory jars.
- **Halloween Stickers and Cutouts:** For decorating Boogey Nightlights and jars. Look for bat, ghost, pumpkin, and spider stickers.
- **Plastic Glow Sticks:** Used in Boogey Nightlights for a glowing effect. Ensure the glow sticks are non-toxic and safe for children.
- **Plastic Beads, Gems, or Foam Beads:** Small, colorful decorations to hide in the slime for sensory play.
- **Candy Eyes and Sprinkles:** For decorating Monster Marshmallow Pops and edible treats.
- **Silicone Molds:** Use Halloween-themed silicone molds for shaping gelatin-based treats into spooky forms.

4. Cleaning and Safety Supplies

- **Hand Wipes or Damp Cloths:** For cleaning hands before and after slime play.
- **Vinegar and Rubbing Alcohol:** Useful for cleaning up slime stains on surfaces and clothing.
- **Washcloths:** For wiping down surfaces during and after crafting.
- **Airtight Storage Containers:** Essential for keeping slime fresh and preventing it from drying out.

Where to Buy

Recommendations for Safe and Child-Friendly Supplies

Finding **safe, child-friendly supplies** is essential when making slime, crafts, and snacks. Below is a list of recommended places where you can purchase the supplies needed for all the activities in this book:

1. Craft Stores

- **Michaels:** A great source for craft supplies like glue, glitter, decorative beads, food coloring, and plastic decorations. They often have holiday-themed items, making it easy to find Halloween stickers, cookie cutters, and molds.
- **Joann Fabrics and Crafts:** Offers a wide selection of crafting tools, glow sticks, plastic jars, stickers, and hot glue guns.
- **Hobby Lobby:** A one-stop shop for crafting materials, including paints, jars, glitter, and storage containers. They carry seasonal decorations that are perfect for Halloween crafts.

2. Supermarkets and Grocery Stores

- **Walmart:** A convenient place to find both crafting supplies (glue, baking soda, cornstarch) and edible ingredients (gelatin, marshmallows, powdered sugar). Walmart also carries kitchen tools like mixing bowls, cookie cutters, and plastic trays.

- **Target:** Stock up on basic slime ingredients, candy melts, marshmallows, and kitchen tools. They often carry seasonal items, including glow-in-the-dark supplies.
- **Local Grocery Stores:** Great for picking up pantry items like cornstarch, gelatin, powdered sugar, and food coloring. Most grocery stores also carry basic kitchen tools like measuring cups and mixing bowls.

3. Online Retailers

- **Amazon:** For the convenience of online shopping, Amazon offers a wide range of crafting supplies, including non-toxic glues, glow-in-the-dark powders, candy eyes, and food-grade glitter. Look for child-friendly and non-toxic products when purchasing ingredients and decorations.
- **Etsy:** A fantastic resource for unique, handmade decorations, stickers, and themed molds. You can find specialized craft supplies like Halloween-themed cookie cutters and silicone molds.
- **Bulk Craft Stores (e.g., Discount School Supply):** Perfect for buying crafting supplies in bulk, especially if you're planning activities for classroom events or parties.

4. Dollar Stores

- **Dollar Tree:** Budget-friendly source for basic crafting supplies like plastic containers, jars, lollipop sticks, and plastic tablecloths. They often carry seasonal items for Halloween, such as stickers and small trinkets for slime play.
- **Dollar General:** Another cost-effective option for picking up items like mixing bowls, plastic trays, and small decorations.

5. Specialty Baking Stores

- **Baking Supply Stores:** Visit specialty baking stores for food-grade glitter, candy melts, cookie cutters, and decorative candies used in Monster Marshmallow Pops and Boogey Goo Treats.

6. Crafting and Cooking Supply Websites

- **Wilton:** Ideal for purchasing high-quality candy eyes, sprinkles, and silicone molds for creating edible treats.
- **Oriental Trading:** Offers a wide variety of themed stickers, plastic trinkets, and decorations suitable for children's crafts.

Tips for Buying Supplies:

- **Look for Non-Toxic Labels:** Ensure all ingredients, especially glue, paint, glitter, and food coloring, are labeled as non-toxic and safe for children.
- **Check Expiration Dates:** When buying food-based items like gelatin, candy melts, and marshmallows, always check the expiration dates to ensure they're fresh.
- **Read Product Descriptions:** When shopping online, read product descriptions carefully to ensure the items meet safety and age-appropriate guidelines.

By gathering these supplies and ingredients, you'll be fully equipped to create the spooky, gooey, and tasty fun outlined in this book. Whether you're shopping online or visiting your local craft store, this list and guide will help you stock up on everything needed for a safe and memorable adventure in the Boogey World!

Chapter 9: Printable Extras

Welcome to the **Printable Extras** chapter! This section is packed with creative and practical printables to enhance your Boogey World crafting adventures. Whether you're storing slime, organizing your crafting supplies, or adding some extra fun with coloring pages, these printables will make your Boogey-themed activities even more memorable. This chapter includes **Boogey Goo Labels** for slime storage, **Activity Sheets** featuring coloring pages and bingo cards, and a **Crafting Checklist** to help parents and teachers prepare for slime-making and spooky crafts. Let's explore each printable in detail!

Boogey Goo Labels
Cute Labels for Storing Slime

One of the most fun parts of crafting Boogey Goo is getting to keep and play with it later! To make storage more exciting, you can use these **Boogey Goo Labels** to decorate the containers. These printable labels are designed to give your slime jars a themed look, making them perfect for Halloween parties, classroom events, or gifts.

Label Designs

- **Classic Boogey Goo:** A label featuring a cartoonish, green slime monster with the text "Classic Boogey Goo" in spooky fonts. This is perfect for labeling your classic glue-based slime containers.
- **Glow-in-the-Dark Slime:** A glowing label with a moon and stars, reading "Glow-in-the-Dark Boogey Goo." Use this label for your slime that glows under the dark, adding a mystical vibe to your jars.
- **Oobleck:** A playful label with swirling colors, stating "Oobleck Goo." Great for labeling containers filled with cornstarch-based oobleck.

- **Fluffy Slime:** A fluffy cloud design with the words "Fluffy Boogey Goo." Use this label for the baking soda and conditioner-based slime.
- **Edible Slime:** A fun, snack-themed label reading "Edible Boogey Goo – Safe to Eat!" Clearly marks containers that hold gelatin or marshmallow-based slime so children know it's safe to taste.

How to Use the Labels

1. **Print:** Print the Boogey Goo Labels on sticker paper or regular paper and use double-sided tape to attach them to your containers.
2. **Cut:** Use scissors to carefully cut out each label. You can choose to print labels in different sizes to fit various container shapes.
3. **Attach:** Stick the labels onto your slime storage containers, jars, or bags. Make sure to press down firmly so they adhere securely.
4. **Personalize:** If you want to add a personal touch, use a pen or marker to write the date the slime was made or the name of the child who created it on the label.

Tip: Laminate the labels if you plan on using them for multiple batches of slime. This way, they can be reused by simply sticking them onto new containers with removable tape.

Activity Sheets

Halloween-Themed Coloring Pages, Bingo Cards, and Sensory Play Prompts

Printable **Activity Sheets** are a fantastic way to keep kids entertained while waiting for their slime to form or as a fun break between crafts. This section provides a variety of activity sheets, including Halloween-themed coloring pages, Boogey Bingo cards, and sensory play prompts.

1. Halloween-Themed Coloring Pages

- **Boogey Creatures:** Printable coloring pages featuring friendly boogey monsters, ghosts, pumpkins, and bats. These illustrations are perfect for kids of all ages to color with crayons, markers, or colored pencils.
- **Slime Monsters:** Pages depicting cartoon slime monsters oozing out of jars. Kids can color the monsters in their favorite spooky shades, adding glitter or stickers for extra flair.
- **Haunted House:** A scene showing a haunted house surrounded by slime and creepy trees. Children can color and add their own spooky details to make the picture come to life.
- **Glow-in-the-Dark Fun:** Print these pages on regular paper and color them with glow-in-the-dark markers or crayons. They'll create an eerie glow when the lights go out!

2. Boogey Bingo Cards

- **Boogey Bingo:** Create a Halloween-themed bingo game with printable **Boogey Bingo Cards**. Each card has a 5x5 grid filled with spooky icons like spiders, pumpkins, cauldrons, bats, and the Boogeyman himself.
- **Caller Sheet:** A separate printable page featuring small versions of the icons used on the bingo cards. Cut them out, fold them, and place them in a small bowl for drawing during the game.
- **Markers:** Print small, square markers with Halloween-themed designs (like mini pumpkins, spiders, or candy corn) that players can use to mark their cards during the game.

3. Sensory Play Prompts

- **Rescue the Bug:** A prompt card encouraging kids to dig through their slime to find and "rescue" the hidden plastic bugs. Includes playful instructions and illustrations of bugs peeking out of slime.
- **Find the Gems:** A sensory play card with prompts for kids to find hidden gems within their goo. The card includes a mini checklist for kids to tick off each gem as they find it.
- **Sculpt and Shape:** A printable card with ideas for sculpting different shapes and creatures using fluffy slime. The card has fun illustrations of bats, ghosts, and pumpkins to inspire kids during their playtime.

How to Use: Print the activity sheets and distribute them during playtime. You can use them as a structured activity or a fun, free-play option for kids to explore their creativity.

Crafting Checklist
A Printable Checklist for Boogey Crafting Days

Preparation is the key to a smooth crafting day. The **Crafting Checklist** helps parents, teachers, and caregivers gather all necessary materials and ingredients in advance, ensuring that each Boogey craft session runs seamlessly. The checklist is divided into sections based on the types of activities you'll be creating, including slime-making, snacks, games, and crafts.

Checklist Categories

1. **Slime Supplies:** A list of ingredients and tools needed for various slime recipes:
   - White school glue
   - Baking soda
   - Cornstarch
   - Hair conditioner
   - Contact lens solution
   - Food coloring
   - Mixing bowls, measuring cups, spatulas
2. **Crafting Tools:** Essential items for crafting Boogey Jars, Night-lights, and Footprints:
   - Clear plastic or glass jars
   - Paintbrushes
   - Plastic spiders and trinkets
   - Glow sticks
   - Plastic tablecloths, scissors, tape
3. **Edible Treats:** Items needed for making Monster Marshmallow Pops and Boogey Goo Treats:
   - Marshmallows
   - Gelatin
   - Candy melts
   - Lollipop sticks

- ○ Edible glitter and sprinkles
4. **Activity Sheets and Labels:** What to print before starting:
    - ○ Boogey Goo Labels
    - ○ Coloring pages
    - ○ Bingo cards
    - ○ Sensory play prompts
5. **Clean-Up Supplies:** Tools to make clean-up easy:
    - ○ Hand wipes
    - ○ Vinegar (for removing slime stains)
    - ○ Resealable bags
    - ○ Storage containers for slime

How to Use the Checklist:

1. **Print:** Print the checklist and place it in a visible location, such as on the fridge or crafting area.
2. **Prepare:** Before your crafting day, gather the items listed on the checklist. Use the checkboxes to mark off each item as you go.
3. **Stay Organized:** Refer to the checklist throughout your crafting session to keep everything on track.

Tip: Laminate the checklist for reusable use. You can use a dry-erase marker to check off items each time you plan a Boogey crafting day.

These **printable extras** add an extra layer of organization and fun to your Boogey World adventures. From cute labels for slime jars to activity sheets that spark creativity, and a comprehensive crafting checklist to keep you organized, these printables ensure every crafting day is both enjoyable and stress-free. Print, prepare, and get ready for hours of gooey, spooky fun!

All can be found at ApophisEnterpriseLLC.org/Apophisemporiumshop

Conclusion

As we reach the end of our Boogey World adventure, it's time to reflect on all the fun, creativity, and spookiness we've explored together! You've learned how to craft gooey slimes, make eerie crafts, and even whip up tasty treats that capture the essence of Halloween magic. This book is more than just a guide; it's an invitation to enter a world of imagination, laughter, and a little bit of mischief. Let's wrap up with some final thoughts and encouragement to continue the fun well beyond the pages.

Wrap-Up and Encouragement

Congratulations! You've unlocked the secrets of Boogey Goo and ventured deep into a realm of gooey crafts, spooky games, and delicious treats. This book was designed to spark creativity, encourage sensory play, and help families make lasting memories during the Halloween season. We hope that you and your little ones had a blast experimenting with different slime recipes, creating glowing nightlights, and crafting eerie snacks.

But remember, the fun doesn't have to stop here! The activities and crafts you've learned in this book can be enjoyed all year round. Halloween may come and go, but the magic of creative play and exploration is timeless. Here are some words of encouragement as you continue your journey:

- **Embrace Creativity:** Encourage your children to use their imaginations when crafting their Boogey creations. Whether they're sculpting a new slime monster, decorating a glow-in-the-dark jar, or inventing a spooky story to go along with their slime, every activity offers an opportunity to think outside the box.
- **Get Messy:** Don't worry about the mess; it's all part of the fun! Some of the best memories are made when hands are sticky with slime or the kitchen is filled with the scent of marshmallow treats. Embrace the messiness of playtime, knowing that clean-up is just another part of the adventure.

- **Create New Traditions:** Use these activities to establish new family traditions for Halloween or even weekly crafting sessions. The joy of mixing slime, crafting Boogey jars, and playing spooky games can become a cherished tradition that your kids will look forward to every year.
- **Adapt and Expand:** Feel free to modify and expand on the recipes and crafts in this book. If your child has a new idea for a Boogey snack or a slime variation, give it a try! Part of the magic is in experimenting, learning, and making each experience uniquely your own.

Above all, have fun! Halloween is a season for laughter, mystery, and creativity, and this book has given you a treasure trove of activities to celebrate the spooky season in a way that's enjoyable and memorable. So go ahead—mix up a new batch of Boogey Goo, craft some glowing nightlights, and fill your home with laughter and the magic of play!

Share Your Boogey Goo Creations!

Your Boogey World journey is unique, and we'd love to see the creativity and fun you and your little ones have brought to life! Sharing your experiences not only spreads the joy but also inspires other families to join in on the gooey fun. Here's how you can share your Boogey creations and be part of our spooky community:

Share on Social Media

- **Post Your Photos:** Capture the excitement of crafting and playing with your Boogey Goo, snacks, and Halloween crafts. Whether it's a spooky jar filled with glow-in-the-dark slime, a Boogeyman hide-and-seek adventure, or a batch of Monster Marshmallow Pops, snap some photos to show off your creations!
- **Use Our Hashtag:** To connect with other Boogey World adventurers, use the hashtag **#BoogeyGooFun** when you post your photos on social media. This way, everyone can see your brilliant ideas and join in on the fun.

- **Tag Us:** If there's a social media page or community associated with this book, be sure to tag us in your posts! We'd love to showcase some of the most creative, spooky, and fun-filled Boogey creations on our page.

Engage with the Community

- **Comment and Share:** Follow the hashtag **#BoogeyGooFun** to see what other families are creating. Comment on their posts, share ideas, and even learn new twists on the activities you've enjoyed.
- **Participate in Challenges:** Keep an eye out for seasonal challenges or contests where you can submit your Boogey Goo creations for a chance to win fun prizes and connect with other crafty parents and kids.

By sharing your Boogey Goo experiences, you help build a community of creativity, fun, and a little bit of Halloween magic. Plus, seeing everyone's different takes on the activities can inspire new ideas for your next crafting day!

Final Thoughts

The Boogey World is a place of endless possibilities. With each new batch of slime, each craft project, and every spooky snack, you've added a touch of magic to the Halloween season. As you continue exploring, remember that creativity has no limits. Whether you're crafting a new type of Boogey Goo, inventing a fresh game, or cooking up a gooey treat, the joy is in the making, sharing, and playing.

So here's to more messy, squishy, and imaginative days ahead. Let the spirit of the Boogey World linger in your home, filling it with laughter, fun, and the excitement of discovery. Happy crafting, happy playing, and most of all, **Happy Halloween!** ◇

Now, it's time to grab your slime, put on your crafting hats, and let the Boogey magic continue! Don't forget to share your creations with the world using **#BoogeyGooFun**, and let's keep the spooky celebration going all season long!

<u>Appendices</u>

Welcome to the Appendices section, where we provide additional resources to support your Boogey World adventures! Here you'll find a **Glossary of Terms** that explains key words and concepts related to slime-making, sensory play, and crafting. We've also included a **FAQs** section to address common questions about slime safety, storage, and alternative ingredients. This section is a handy reference to help ensure your Boogey crafting experiences are safe, fun, and educational.

Glossary of Terms

Key Terms Related to Slime-Making and Sensory Play

Activator: An ingredient that changes the chemical properties of glue to form slime. In most slime recipes, the activator is contact lens solution containing boric acid or sodium borate. The activator binds the polymer chains in the glue, creating the stretchy, gooey texture of slime.

Baking Soda: A common household ingredient used in slime recipes to alter the texture of the slime. When combined with an activator like contact lens solution, it helps thicken the slime, giving it structure and making it less sticky.

Borax: A mineral and a key ingredient in some slime activators. It is often mixed with water to create a slime activator, although many modern recipes use alternatives like contact lens solution for a safer, child-friendly option.

Cornstarch: A fine, powdery substance used in some slime recipes, such as oobleck. When mixed with water, it forms a non-Newtonian fluid, giving the slime its unique texture. Cornstarch is also used to make edible slime, as it thickens mixtures and adds stretchiness.

Edible Slime: A type of slime made using food-safe ingredients, such as gelatin, marshmallows, cornstarch, or pudding mix. Edible slime is safe for young children who may put items in their mouths, making it an excellent option for sensory play.

Food Coloring: Non-toxic dyes used to add vibrant colors to slime, making it more visually appealing. Food coloring comes in liquid, gel, or powder forms and can be mixed to create custom colors.

Glow-in-the-Dark Powder/Paint: A non-toxic, luminescent material used to make slime glow in the dark. When added to slime, this powder or paint absorbs light and releases it as a glow when the lights are turned off, creating a magical effect.

Non-Newtonian Fluid: A fluid whose viscosity (thickness) changes under stress or force. Oobleck, a mixture of cornstarch and water, is an example of a non-Newtonian fluid. When you apply pressure to oobleck, it acts like a solid, but when you let it sit or move slowly, it behaves like a liquid.

Oobleck: A simple slime made from a mixture of cornstarch and water. Named after a substance in a Dr. Seuss book, oobleck is a non-Newtonian fluid that can be both solid and liquid, depending on the pressure applied to it. It's often used in sensory play and science experiments.

Polyvinyl Acetate (PVA) Glue: The main ingredient in most slime recipes, commonly known as school glue or white glue. PVA glue contains molecules that link together when mixed with an activator, forming the stretchy, gooey texture of slime.

Sensory Play: Activities that engage a child's senses (touch, sight, sound, smell, and sometimes taste) to help develop cognitive, motor, and social skills. Slime-making is a popular sensory play activity because it allows children to explore textures, colors, and movement through touch and manipulation.

Stretchiness: A key characteristic of slime that determines how far it can be stretched without breaking. Stretchiness can be adjusted by varying the amount of activator or by adding ingredients like lotion or conditioner to soften the slime.

Thickening Agent: A substance that helps give slime its desired consistency. In slime recipes, baking soda, cornstarch, and powdered sugar (in edible slime) are common thickening agents that help bind ingredients together.

Washable Glue: A type of school glue that is safe, non-toxic, and easily washable from surfaces, skin, and fabrics. It is the main ingredient in many child-friendly slime recipes.

FAQs

Common Questions About Slime Safety, Storage, and Alternatives

Q1: Is slime safe for young children to play with?

- **A:** Most slime recipes in this book use non-toxic ingredients and are generally safe for older children. However, for younger children who may put things in their mouths, it's best to use **edible slime recipes** made with food-safe ingredients like marshmallows, cornstarch, and gelatin. Always supervise children during slime play to ensure they don't ingest non-edible slime or decorations.

Q2: What should I do if slime gets on clothes or furniture?

- **A:** If slime gets on clothing, let it dry, then scrape off as much as possible. For any remaining residue, soak the stained area in a mixture of warm water and vinegar before washing. For furniture, use a damp cloth with warm, soapy water to blot the area. Rubbing alcohol can help remove stubborn slime from hard surfaces.

Q3: How long does homemade slime last?

- **A:** The shelf life of homemade slime varies depending on the recipe:
    - **Glue-Based Slime:** Can last for several weeks if stored in an airtight container.
    - **Oobleck:** Best used the day it's made, but can be stored for up to 24 hours in a sealed container.
    - **Fluffy Baking Soda Slime:** Typically lasts about a week when stored properly.
    - **Edible Slimes:** Shorter shelf life (1–2 days) and should be refrigerated.

Q4: How should I store slime to keep it fresh?

- **A:** Store slime in an **airtight container** or resealable plastic bag to prevent it from drying out. Keep the container in a **cool, dry place**, away from direct sunlight or heat sources. For edible slime, store it in the refrigerator.

Q5: What if my slime is too sticky?

- **A:** If your slime is too sticky, try adding a small amount of **baking soda** or a few drops of **contact lens solution** (if the recipe includes glue). Knead the slime thoroughly to incorporate the extra ingredient. For fluffy slime, adding more conditioner can also help reduce stickiness.

Q6: Can I use something other than contact lens solution as an activator?

- **A:** Yes! While contact lens solution is a popular and child-safe activator, you can also use:
    - **Liquid Starch:** Commonly used as a laundry additive, liquid starch can activate glue-based slime.
    - **Borax Solution:** Dissolve 1 teaspoon of borax powder in 1 cup of warm water. Slowly add the solution to the glue mixture to create slime. (Note: Always use caution with borax, as it can irritate the skin if not diluted properly. Supervise children closely when using this ingredient.)

Q7: How can I make my slime stretchier?

- **A:** To make your slime stretchier, add a small amount of **lotion** or **hair conditioner** to the mixture and knead it in. You can also reduce the amount of activator (contact lens solution) used to create a softer, more flexible slime.

Q8: What can I do if my slime dries out?

- **A:** If your slime starts to dry out, try adding a few drops of **warm water** or **lotion** and knead the slime until it regains its original texture. For glue-based slime, adding a bit of contact lens solution can help revive its stretchiness.

Q9: Are there any alternatives for children with sensitive skin?

- **A:** For children with sensitive skin, consider using **edible slime recipes** made with safe ingredients like cornstarch, marshmallows, or gelatin. Avoid slimes that contain harsh chemicals or artificial colors, and always perform a patch test on the inner wrist to check for any reactions before extended play.

Q10: Can I add essential oils to my slime for fragrance?

- **A:** Yes, you can add a few drops of **essential oil** to give your slime a pleasant scent. However, use caution and choose oils that are safe for children, such as lavender or chamomile. Always use essential oils sparingly, as some children may be sensitive to strong fragrances.

Q11: Is glow-in-the-dark slime safe?

- **A:** Yes, glow-in-the-dark slime can be safe if you use non-toxic, child-friendly **glow-in-the-dark powder** or paint specifically designed for crafting. Ensure that children do not ingest the slime and supervise them during play.

Q12: What if I don't have food coloring?

- **A:** If you don't have food coloring, you can try using **washable paints** to color your slime. For edible slime, you can use **natural food colorings** like beet juice, turmeric, or cocoa powder.

By referring to this glossary and FAQs section, you can navigate your Boogey Goo crafting adventures with confidence, safety, and a better understanding of how to make the most of your slime-making experience. Whether you're troubleshooting a sticky batch of slime or looking for ingredient alternatives, these resources will help you keep the gooey fun going!

<u>Message from the Author:</u>

I hope you enjoyed this book, I love astrology and knew there was not a book such as this out on the shelf. I love metaphysical items as well. Please check out my other books:

-Life of Government Benefits

-My life of Hell

-My life with Hydrocephalus

-Red Sky

-World Domination:Woman's rule

-World Domination:Woman's Rule 2: The War

-Life and Banishment of Apophis: book 1

-The Kidney Friendly Diet

-The Ultimate Hemp Cookbook

-Creating a Dispensary(legally)

-Cleanliness throughout life: the importance of showering from childhood to adulthood.

-Strong Roots: The Risks of Overcoddling children

-Hemp Horoscopes: Cosmic Insights and Earthly Healing

- Celestial Hemp Navigating the Zodiac: Through the Green Cosmos

-Astrological Hemp: Aligning The Stars with Earth's Ancient Herb

-The Astrological Guide to Hemp: Stars, Signs, and Sacred Leaves

-Green Growth: Innovative Marketing Strategies for your Hemp Products and Dispensary

-Cosmic Cannabis

-Astrological Munchies

-Henry The Hemp

-Zodiacal Roots: The Astrological Soul Of Hemp

- Green Constellations: Intersection of Hemp and Zodiac

-Hemp in The Houses: An astrological Adventure Through The Cannabis Galaxy

-Galactic Ganja Guide

Heavenly Hemp

Zodiac Leaves

Doctor Who Astrology

Cannastrology

Stellar Satvias and Cosmic Indicas

<u>Celestial Cannabis: A Zodiac Journey</u>

AstroHerbology: The Sky and The Soil: Volume 1

AstroHerbology:Celestial Cannabis:Volume 2

Cosmic Cannabis Cultivation

The Starry Guide to Herbal Harmony: Volume 1

The Starry Guide to Herbal Harmony: Cannabis Universe: Volume 2

Yugioh Astrology: Astrological Guide to Deck, Duels and more

Nightmare Mansion: Echoes of The Abyss

Nightmare Mansion 2: Legacy of Shadows

Nightmare Mansion 3: Shadows of the Forgotten

Nightmare Mansion 4: Echoes of the Damned

The Life and Banishment of Apophis: Book 2

Nightmare Mansion: Halls of Despair

<u>Healing with Herb: Cannabis and Hydrocephalus</u>

<u>Planetary Pot: Aligning with Astrological Herbs: Volume 1</u>

Fast Track to Freedom: 30 Days to Financial Independence Using AI, Assets, and Agile Hustles

<u>Cosmic Hemp Pathways</u>

How to Become Financially Free in 30 Days: 10,000 Paths to Prosperity

Zodiacal Herbage: Astrological Insights: Volume 1

Nightmare Mansion: Whispers in the Walls

The Daleks Invade Atlantis

Henry the hemp and Hydrocephalus

10X The Kidney Friendly Diet

Cannabis Universe: Adult coloring book

Hemp Astrology: The Healing Power of the Stars

Zodiacal Herbage: Astrological Insights: Cannabis Universe: Volume 2

<u>Planetary Pot: Aligning with Astrological Herbs: Cannabis Universes: Volume 2</u>

Doctor Who Meets the Replicators and SG-1: The Ultimate Battle for Survival

Nightmare Mansion: Curse of the Blood Moon

<u>The Celestial Stoner: A Guide to the Zodiac</u>

Cosmic Pleasures: Sex Toy Astrology for Every Sign

Hydrocephalus Astrology: Navigating the Stars and Healing Waters

Lapis and the Mischievous Chocolate Bar

Celestial Positions: Sexual Astrology for Every Sign

Apophis's Shadow Work Journal: : A Journey of Self-Discovery and Healing

Kinky Cosmos: Sexual Kink Astrology for Every Sign

Digital Cosmos: The Astrological Digimon Compendium

Stellar Seeds: The Cosmic Guide to Growing with Astrology

Apophis's Daily Gratitude Journal

Cat Astrology: Feline Mysteries of the Cosmos

The Cosmic Kama Sutra: An Astrological Guide to Sexual Positions

Unleash Your Potential: A Guided Journal Powered by AI Insights

Whispers of the Enchanted Grove

Cosmic Pleasures: An Astrological Guide to Sexual Kinks

369, 12 Manifestation Journal

Whisper of the nocturne journal(blank journal for writing or drawing)

The Boogey Book

Locked In Reflection: A Chastity Journey Through Locktober

Generating Wealth Quickly:

How to Generate $100,000 in 24 Hours

Star Magic: Harness the Power of the Universe

The Flatulence Chronicles: A Fart Journal for Self-Discovery

The Doctor and The Death Moth

Seize the Day: A Personal Seizure Tracking Journal

The Ultimate Boogeyman Safari: A Journey into the Boogie World and Beyond

Whispers of Samhain: 1,000 Spells of Love, Luck, and Lunar Magic: Samhain Spell Book

Apophis's guides:

Witch's Spellbook Crafting Guide for Halloween

<u>Frost & Flame: The Enchanted Yule Grimoire of 1000 Winter Spells</u>

Get Some Tarot cards: https://www.makeplayingcards.com/sell/apophis-occult-shop

Get some shirts: https://www.bonfire.com/store/apophis-shirt-emporium/

<u>Instagrams:</u>
@apophis_enterprises,
@apophisbookemporium,
@apophisscardshop
Twitter: @apophisenterpr1
Tiktok:@apophisenterprise
Youtube: @sg1fan23477

Podcast: Apophis Chat Zone: https://open.spotify.com/show/5zXbrCLEV2xzCp8ybrfHsk?si=fb4d4fdbdce44dec

 –

Newsletter: https://apophiss-newsletter-27c897.beehiiv.com/

www.ingramcontent.com/pod-product-compliance
Lightning Source LLC
Chambersburg PA
CBHW072116150726
47999CB00005B/2023